SELL PHOTOS ONLINE

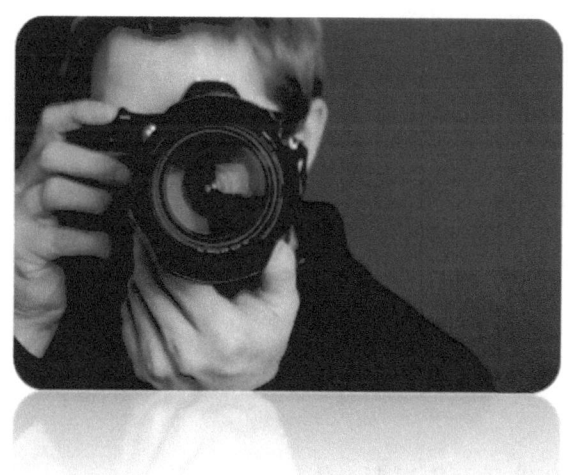

Make money from your digital
camera on Microstock sites

Stephen Wilson

ISBN: 978-0-557-11455-9

Preface

This book is dedicated to the millions of talented individuals around the world whose work is creating the new world of digital media. While photography was the first creative media to adopt this concept, digital media is changing the role of the "amateur" in worlds as diverse as music, graphic arts, and writing. Web storefronts such as IStockphoto, Amazon, Shutterstock and scores of others are providing a new outlet for creative individuals to reach new audiences worldwide.

This digital phenomenon lets anyone showcase their abilities and market their artist talent as far as the Internet can reach. For the first time in human history, we all have the opportunity to be seen, heard, and prosper in the global marketplace. I hope this book helps you in creating your new, limitless future with digital photography.

Acknowledgements

The author wishes to thank David Lewis and the many other IStockphoto photographers who were resources for this book.

Contents

1

Forward

The Web's widely-read and trusted independent tutorial author teaches you how to upload and begin selling your photos and videos today! Learn the insider's tips for working with IStockphoto, Shutterstock and all the other microstock agencies that put money in your pocket! Economic security for your family at the *Click of a Camera*!

Since 2004, Stephen Wilson's blog, "Basic Marketing" has been helping small businesses find new and innovative ways to help companies succeed in marketplace. Now he turns his attention to the exciting world of digital media. Using clear, easy-to-understand language, the author gives you simple directions for starting a new and profitable sideline.

Wilson's perspective is unique since he comes from a career in advertising. He has purchased hundreds of stock photographs, so he knows what captures the eye of the buyer. He shares this experience with you, showing you how to consider your photos from the buyer's perspective, helping you to increase sales and your income.

Additionally, Wilson profiles David Lewis, one of IStockphoto's most successful photographers. Three years ago, as a supplement to his full time job, Lewis began taking photos to submit online. Today, he makes over *$50,000 per year* in additional income. You'll love hearing how Lewis changed his life with his digital camera. You could be next!

Got a good video camera at home? This is your chance to make money with your video talent by submitting footage to the online marketplace. It's a growing field providing great opportunities for newcomers. Wilson covers this field as well.

"*Wilson's book is helping families gain additional income through digital media. It's a fun, profitable read*," Steve Hubbard, Examiner.com.

2

Let's Get Started

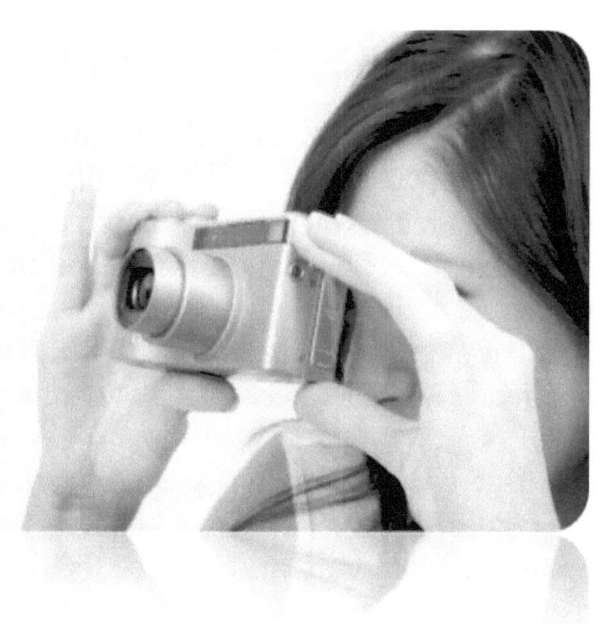

Welcome to the world of digital images! Have you got a good eye and a creative bent? If so, then IStockphoto and the entire world of microstock photography sites can open an exciting, new opportunity to make money during these tough economic times. If you're like me, then you've been amazed by all the stories of people who've made very good money by marketing their products online. Most people can only wish they had an idea or concept that they could sell on the Web and make some of that Internet cash! Well, there's an easy way to get involved with online marketing and all you need is a good quality digital camera (either still or video) and a visually distinctive take on the world around you.

I'm sure you've probably seen all the get-rich-quick scemes that are posted all across the Web. "Start Making Millions Tommorrow" or "How I Retired a Millionaire in 90 Days." Well, I'm sorry to say, those stories aren't real. You'll notice that in my success profile, my friend, David Lewis, is not a millionaire. He makes great additional income, and most people would be thrilled to get it, but he works hard and he posted many, many images to get to his level of success.

But, even if you don't want to work that hard, if you would be happy with a few hundred extra dollars coming in each month this could be the life for you. Do you enjoy taking photos? Are you the one who always takes the camera to the party or to family events? I think that's one of the reasons that most people are successful on IStockphoto. They're doing what they love - taking photos - so it doesn't seem like work. Pretty soon, they have hundreds of photos online, they're making money, and they're hooked. I have found, that in most things, people are talented in the areas that they enjoy the most. So, if you enjoy photography now, you already have an advantage over your competition.

I used to work with amateur photographer David Lewis, he had an office just down the hall from where I was. He always was a multi-talented guy, he was a part-time musician and singer in addition to his "real" job. I remember when he first got involved with IStock. He said that he was worried at first that it was becoming addictive. While at work, he kept logging on to his account several times each day to see how many photographs he had sold. Well, I think he's gotten a little more use to the "rush" of finding new money in his account each day, but for most of us, it would be quite a thrill. I have one question,however, what do you call an amateur photographer who makes big money on IStockphoto? He still works his regular job (not photography), so is it more accurate to call him a "dual professional"? If so, digital media might be creating an entirely new type of career path for millions of people.

What this Book will do

This is not a photography book. We won't be spending a lot of time talking about lens and lighting, most of this book is about practical matters. How to get up and running fast in the world of microstock. We'll cover topics like:

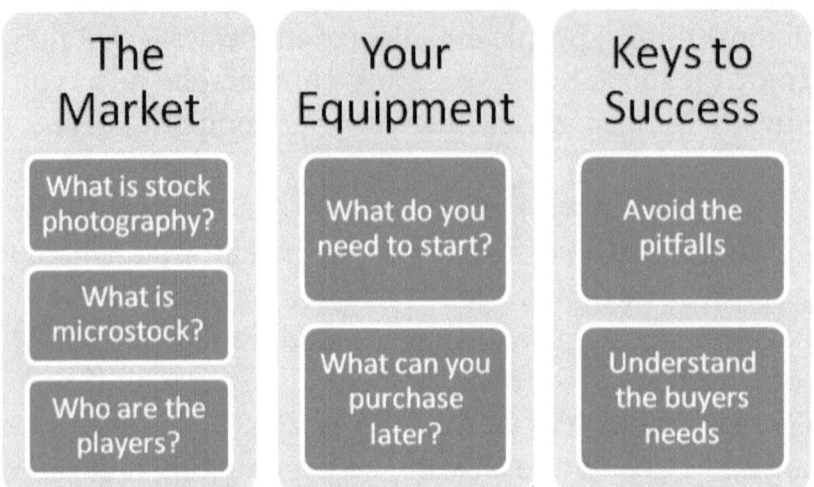

Let's take a look. I think you're going to like this picture!

3

Stock Photography

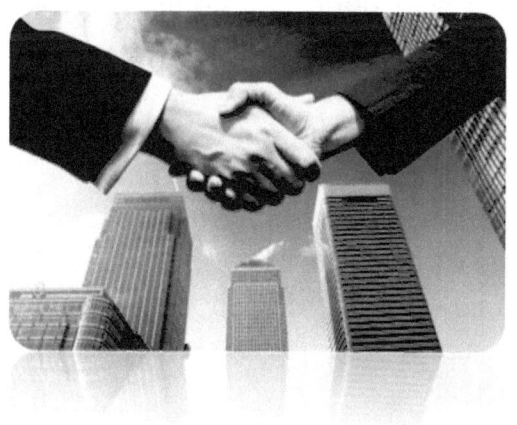

I come from the world of advertising and marketing. I remember the days when we actually hired a photographer for a photo shoot. In a small market, it would cost us at least $1,200 a day for a photographer; and in a large market several times that amount. Even if we chose stock photography, it would cost about $100 or more per photo. If a brochure required 6 to 12 photos, the cost would still be about the same. Marketing departments across America faced the challenge of finding great photographs that they could afford. If you

were a small non-profit, the challenge was even greater. Most non-profits were resigned to using "clip art"
graphics to spice up their printed material.

It was a great time, however, to be a professional
photographer. Professional film equipment was expensive and hard to use. So, why did this make things great
for professional photographers? Well, it made a great
defensive positon. It was very difficult for anyone to
open up shop next door as a competitor. A local amateur photographer, with a day job, who only took
photographs on the weekend for example, could not afford the expensive equipment that would make him or
her any kind of threat to a pro. Even if the amateur did
have the equipment, leaving work to take photographs
in the middle of the day was not an option. Once again,
barriers to market-entry into the professional photography market made life pretty sweet for the full-time
photographer.

But nothing stays the same. A decade or more
ago, when digital cameras started to make their way
into the consumer market, Kodak laughed. They
brushed aside suggestions that digital photography
would continue to improve. Kodak's official stance was
that no one would trust their important family memo-
ries with a technology that had only been around for a
few years. After all, they reasoned, the Kodak name
was synominous with photography.

Serendipitously, at around that same time, that

thing called the Internet was just coming of age. It started off slow and seemed to have few practical applications except for sending eMail. But, it grew fast. As one of the many side effects of digital technology, these two innovations (digital cameras and the Web) make microstock photography possible. As digital camera quality increased (and prices dropped), the differences between the shots taken by a talented amateur and a professional photographer with thousands upons thousands of dollars of equipment began to lessen. Web speeds increased dramatically, providing the ability to send these photos to an online marketplace.

I remember one argument at the start of one of the last full-blown photo shoots I managed before making the transition to the digital marketplace. The conversation was with a talented professional photographer who saw a pretty bleak future

"The standards have been lowered for photographs," he fumed, as he stormed around my office. "Agencies are looking for photographs that are just "good enough", but not great photographs. They're doing their clients a disservice."

"Are they really?

"Yes, of course," he sputtered. "They should want great photographs. Photography is art!"

"But, they're saving hundreds of dollars", I replied. He stopped and gave me a cold, hard look.

"That shouldn't matter. That shouldn't matter at all," he said.

Well, as we know, money does matter and it opened up the stock photography market to talented amateurs. IStockphoto was the first to really leverage the power of digital images delieved via the Web to create a new sales category called Microstock. Today, there are many competitors to IStockphoto and they're all seeking your photographs. They can't survive without you!

Why is this form of stock photography called microstock? Because the payment is really "micro" in comparison to the giant size payments to buy the publication rights to traditonal stock photography. I know, I know, bad joke. I'm sure, at first, even IStockphoto didn't really see the potential of this market. In the beginning, they were targeting all the small businesses and non-profits who couldn't afford the price of either a professional photographer or good stock photography. The market, however, is huge. Small businesses make up the lion share of businesses in the United States. Worldwide, the story is the same. Small business is what makes the world economy run.

A funny thing happened along the way to serving the small business market with photography. Many of the large businesses in America began to take a hard look at their photography costs. Why were they spending 20 times or more that small business was paying for photography? Over the protests of agency art directors, stock photography took on a greater role in advertising and media.Today, everyone who loves is looking for stock photography begins their search at a microstock agency like IStockphoto or Shutterstock. Only with great reluctance will an agency, large corporation, or small business turn to a professional photographer. The world has opened up for a talented amateur with a camera. Just the over day, I saw an image of a senior couple being used on a display at a bus stop. It's the same image that's used in this book. There's nothing really remarkable about the image, but it sells an idea clearly and simply. That's the secret behind photography that sells and we'll be discussing that important concept later in the book.

Insider Tip #1: I have never seen a shot of two business people shaking hands at the close of a deal that failed to sell multiple times on IStock. If you can do a half-way credible shot of business people closing a deal - there's your first sale. (And you've just justified the cost of this book) In fact, if you want to have the best chance of making money with your photos stick with business subjects – but find a niche! As I look at the business shots on IStock, I see a lot of shots of corporate subjects. Perhaps you can find a niche in certain Mom and Pop businesses. A small retail business will provide many opportunities to create winning shots from both the customer's and business owner's viewpoint.

Making Money with Microstock

Okay, I know what you're thinking; by now, I know microstock photography is sold for less than traditional stock photography, but how much less? Is this really a way to make good money? Depending on the site that you list your images, you'll only make up to a couple of dollars per sale on average. That figure varies according to the image size purchased, whether you list exclusively with an supplier such as IStock and other factors. New pricing models come out all the time with some comeptitors to IStock allowing you to set some limits to your sale.

However, as a general rule, most microstock sales are small. The secret to making money on microstock sites is volume. When you have many, many images listed, you can make significant income through multiple small sales. Microstock can pack a wollop to your wallet when it is delivered via hundreds of small sales.

Remember my friend that I mentioned earlier. David Lewis is making $4 to $5 thousand each month, but it is coming from selling photographs for about $2 each. How does it do it? Two factors ensure his success. Over the past three years he has put almost 3,000 photographs on the IStockphoto site (he lists exclusively there). Additionally, he takes the time to shoot the photos that buyers want. For me, shooting photos that buyers want is the most important factor in your future success. There must be at least a million beautiful shots on all the microstock sites that never sell. The photographer pursued his or her art, but not the potential customer. You can shoot for your portfolio or your pocketbook. An average photo that can be used to sell a product will make more money on IStockphoto than a breathtaking image that can sell a product, service or idea. I will be covering the secrets of shooting what sells later in this book.

If you are tempted to judge the potential of microstock photography right now, remember, just about every business is turning to microstock photography. Each photograph can (and is) sold multiple times. A single image can easily sell hundreds of times and make thousands of dollars over several years time. After you sign up at a few sites, you'll be able to log on to each of these photo sites and see how many times a file has been downloaded. A very popular photo file can be downloaded over 1,000 times! Not bad work for a lazy Saturday afternoon. Will every photo you take sell like that? No, of course not. Pay attention to my insider tips, I'll tell you how the most successful IStockphoto shutterbugs increase their odds.

Also, many sites offer you a greater percentage of the sale if you list exclusively with their site. That might have been a good idea several years ago when microstock was new, but now, the competition is fierce. Most newcomers that I've talked to, report that they make better money by listing on several sites rather than just one. Although those ad hoc reports can't be proven, I tend to agree with their thinking. Some photographers have better luck on some sites compared to others. I don't know if it relates to their shooting style, random luck, or other reasons but some photographers find they have greater sales from the same images posted on (for example) Shutterstock rather than IStockphoto. Of course, the reverse of that example is often the case.

To add to the mystery, some photographers who have the same photos on multiple sites report great success one month on one site compared to others that sell their photos. The next month, sale results might flip around and last month's loser site is now the leader in sales. If you are not exclusive, I think you will have a better chance to have greater consistency in your personal sales from month to month. In my resources section, I will list some blogs from photographers who report their earnings from multiple sites each month. I think you'll be surprised to see the variety of results.

Insider Tip#2: Pick up a brochure from anywhere, selling anything. What kinds of photos are in the brochure? Happy families? Attractive houses? The photos that are in brochures are your cues to subjects that you should be shooting. Houses are always good. Look at the example photo at the beginning of the next chapter. Please note that it's a beautiful day and there's no harsh sunlight reflecting off the front of the house. In real life, this is a very expensive house, but in the world of advertising, this is a middle class home. Although there is a market for upscale photos, more photos are bought to sell products to middle income consumers. Mansions are beautiful, but family homes make a more profitable subject. In regards to shooting homes, always get a property release from the owner and never, ever show an address. Please bear with me, I'll repeat this several times but it's a mistake that many people make over and over again.

Getting Accepted

The most critical time in the process, at IStockphoto or any other microstock agency is during the original application process. At the time of your application you will be asked to submit a certain number of photographs to become a member of that agency. You can become a member at several microstock agencies at the same time, so I recommend that you submit to as many as you can. IStock sometimes has a wait of several weeks before you find out if you've been successful, so submission to more than one company allows you to start submitting to the first company that can process your application and the sooner you start putting your photos online, the sooner you will begin to make money.

You will submit your best photos along with your application. If you are not technically inclined, take the photos that you intend to submit to a local photo shop and ask them to look at them. Store personnel at a camera shop are usually amateur photographers as well and can provide you with valuable insight. They can tell you if there are any problems with the photos that you are submitting that might not be readily visible to the amateur. Don't worry about wasting their time, they should be glad to help. If you become a successful photographer they should see quite a bit of new business each time you walk through the door. They'll be glad to help get you on your way!

Be warned they look very closely at images submitted with applications. A total of three reviews occur at IStock during submission, but each microstock agency has its own procedures. Don't worry, however, each company has a process for resubmission. At IStock, if 2 out of 3 of your photos are accepted, you only have to submit one more, not three different photos. And remember, the evaluators are mostly looking for technical errors at this point with a critical eye to weed out those that will only be tieing up their time with problem photos later. There have been reported cases of judges rejecting images that they feel don't have sufficient commercial possibilities. If that happens to you, don't argue, you won't win. Just find something else to submit.

One important point, don't test their patience. There is a list of photo subjects on the site that they don't want to see – such as shots of flowers. They have enough shots of Roses to last them for decades to come. Don't come across as clueless by submitting shots (no matter how worthy) of the forbidden subjects.

To get ready for your submission process, please have selected at least 10 photos for submission (Shutterstock wants to see 10 different photos, IStock only three). You will also need a scanned copy of your State Driver's Liscense or some other official photo ID.

Passing the Test

Many people simply freak out about the "test" that IStockphoto makes you take before you can become a registered photographer or videographer on their site. It's nothing to be concerned about because you can take the test several times until you pass it. Not only that, but at the time of this writing, it's an open book test. It doesn't really test your knowledge of photography, but simply ensures that you know and understand the rules and regulations on IStockphoto.

Insider Tip #3: It's a numbers game. Don't upload a dozen photos and then stop to "see how you will do". Even the best of the pros need to upload hundreds of photos onto IStock and other sites to make a living. If you can, avoid even thinking about sales until you have at least 100 photos uploaded.

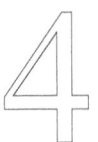

Equipment

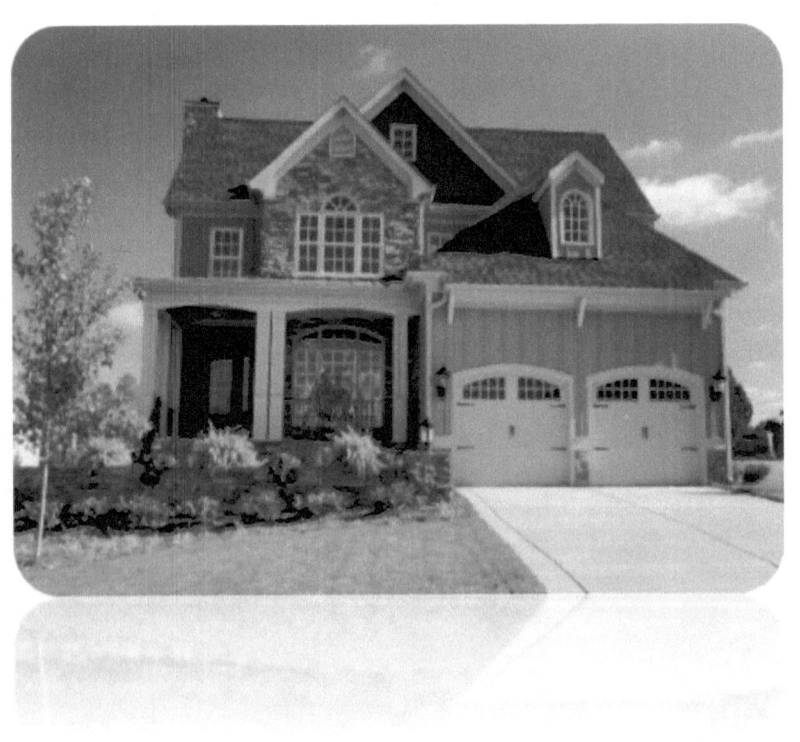

The first question that anyone asks is what kind of equipment do I need? Do I need to get a Nikon with an assortment of lenses? What quality level do the microstock agencies and buyers expect to see from my equipment? How much should I expect to pay for a camera? My advice comes from the standpoint of someone who just wants to make money on IStockphoto. A pro photographer will blanch at these recommendations, but this book is about making money on IStock. If you want to grow in your creativity and develop a side business as a photographer, then there are good reasons to spend money on cameras with all the features. So what's the answer if you just want to start making money fast and not spend a year trying to recoup your investment?

The answer here is relatively straightforward. As the capabilities of digital cameras advance, so do the requirements for digital photo quality at any microstock agency. When IStockphoto first opened its doors (on the Internet) their technical requirements were much less than they are today (both for the quality of the camera and the photographer!). However, we can make the following general recommendations. A four Megapixel Camera or greater should work, but please be aware, the quality standards for microstock continually rise as more and more people submit photos. You don't need to buy additional camera capabilities until you know that the income you will receive from shooting photos will justify the expense.

Don't overspend on a camera - tomorrow there will be a camera which will do more for less money. Cameras are not an investment, they are an expense. I remember my dad handed down an old Hasselblad camera that had been in the family for years. In those days it made sense to hang on to a film camera since film might improve but it could still be used in an old camera. Today, as digital technology improves, there's no way to "stuff" that technology into an old camera. So, the old camera gets suffled off to a desk drawer and the new digital camera becomes the work horse.

Also, forget about brand name cameras. I know that there are folks who are using "off brands" quite easily to submit photographs. Yes, the hard core professional may be able to note minor differences, but not enough to ignore just the right shot for a photo spread.

Special Note: Have a friend with a good camera? Why not borrow it for a weekend and take some shots to submit to IStock. Before you invest in a camera, make sure you like the world of microstock photography.

Another factor that helps to lessen the hard and fast rules about cameras and photo quality is the software known as Photoshop. Most photographs today are subjected to some modifications of some sort of the other. Photos are adjusted in regards to color quality, tone, and cropping. In today's advertising, the photograph is just the starting point for the finished creative. If you provide an art director with just the right look, the right smile, or an original idea, he or she will do the rest. Just be sure to meet the stock agency's mininum image requirements and you'll be fine.

Insider Tip #4: It's not you, it's them. Uploading photos takes an unreal amount of time – far longer than you will be expecting. Most of these sites are working to improve their uploading process, but for now, expect uploading to be a drug. Yes, there is some uploading software you can buy, but once again, my advice is to wait until your sales can help pay for it.

Lighting

One important hurdle to your success on IStock is lighting. If you don't have a professional lighting pack, you *will* have problems with indoor shots. You may have most (if not all) your shots refused for image quality, but it's not your camera, it's your lighting. There are entire books written about three point lighting techniques and they're intimidating for a beginner. So, as always, I'll begin my lighting recommendations from the easiest (and least expensive) solutions

First, take your photos outside to avoid buying lights. I know that's obvious, but there's no reason to rush into the expense of a lighting kit until you begin to earn income from IStock. Let's say you want to start with business shots. Start with a shot of a businessman (or woman) in front of an office building. He or she could be talking on a cell phone, walking with a colleague, the list is endless. For just about any shot you can think of, there's a version of that shot that can be taken outside. Be aware of harsh shadows, but daylight usually provides the kind of general lighting that is perfect for photos and video.

If you simply must shoot indoors, use white foam core to reflect ambient light into your shot. This type of shooting is usually best for product shots (generic products, please) but it can work with faces. Be sure that your talent is not wearing a white shirt – that's too much of a contrast with most skin tones. Be sure to use a big piece of foam core or cardboard to direct as much light as possible on your talent.

For additional light, you can use incandescent work lights (typically used for construction projects) with stands and "bounce" the light off a white ceiling to provide as much general fill as possible. I've seen these low cost options work in a pinch and the reviewer won't know what your light source is.

As you find success on IStockphoto, you can purchase a light kit with stands and filters. Look for used light kits first. These kits are very durable and last for years.

Other equipment

There is a myriad of other types of equipment that

yhou can buy, carts, stands, cases, etc. They all have their uses. For the short term, however, keep your wallet in your pocket. Later on, you can prioritize your purchases according to a purchase justification system. As you consider all your possible choices, choose products that will help you shoot faster and more efficiently. It's a numbers game, increase your numbers and increase your income.

Forget Photoshop (for now)

A lot of people like Photoshop. It's tempting to purchase it to "brush out" logos and correct colors. However, there are many more bad Photoshop examples in the world than good examples. As a beginner, the hours you spend learning Photoshop are taking you away from shooting more images. Remember, uploading images is how you make money.

Insider Tip #5 Sign up for Newsletters. Almost all online photo and video Websites offer monthly newsletters. They all offer valuable insight into what topics are selling, how to get your photos noticed by buyers and other tips to make you more successful. Be sure to sign up for these helpful monthly newsletters, they will help you turn your new hobby into new profits.

5

Shooting Video for IStockphoto

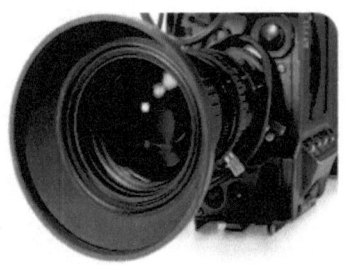

Video is growing in importance as a communication tool on the Web. Google recognizes the user preference for videos and tries to return results from YouTube for every match in keyword. Most Websites now feature videos as part of product demos, "how tos", or to illustrate difficult concepts. With today's multi-clutural society, videos (which marry image and narrative) are a great way to create an easy to understand message with an audience that may speak English as a second language. Also, video messages help circumvent the ever-shrinking literacy levels in this country.Video is a way to help native speakers who might have difficulty following along with dense text-only explanations. With greater Internet speeds, it seems video has a strong future on the Web.

It's no wonder then that the demand for stock video has grown sharply. Most families have some type of video camera so it seems like this is a natural expansion of your submissions to Istock

There are some considerations to keep in mind: Some new cameras don't use a tape at all. They compress video to store in all on the camera's memory. The problem, however, comes with compression. It can cause some glitches (called artifacts) that are sometimes impossible to see, except by a technician. These artifacts can cause your videos to be rejected. Many of the pocket video cameras (Flip and others) cause these artifacts to occur. If possible, you are better off purchasing the older style cameras that still use a video tape rather than a chip since there is less chance of technical flaws.

Another factor is our transition to from the old NTSC signal to High Definition television. Fortuantely, for now at least, you can submit both formats for Web video. These are both acceptable, although the High Definition videos are priced higher than older NTSC formats. The cheaper NTSC formats, however, can sell more frequently. Typically, businesses are buying video for short term use and are not as concerned about the format for a Web video that will probably have a life span of only a few months.

One thing that I'm sure that you'll immediately notice is that the sale price of a 30 second (or less) shot is much higher than for still images. The downside is that the video market is much smaller compared to the photography market and videos sell much less frequently than still photos. Most videographers who are shooting video post their videos on multiple sites in order to catch stray buyers.

If you're a beginner, here are some pointers that will get you up and running fast with IStockphoto:

First, just like photos, be sure that you're aware of logos that may enter or leave your scene as your shoot. Remember, a video shot with a logo will get rejected just as quickly as a still image. This means that you'll have to pay attention to your changing background if your shoot outside. Did that truck that drove by in the far distance have a company name blazoned on its side? Did you pan by a bill board or store sign – that will kill a sale. Video captures 30 frames per second and it multiplies the chances that a logo might slip by in the background when your attention is on the action in the foreground.

If you're a beginner in videography, you'll definetly need a tripod. If you've had more experience - - *you'll still need a tripod.* IStock wants every shot to be captured from a tripod (unless the shot is meant for some artistic purpose. Don't think you can "fool" the review process by remaining very still with a shoulder mounted camera. You just can't fool the judges and you don't want to waste a day of photography by having every shot rejected because you didn't use a tripod.

Much like when you are shooting still images, be sure that you have sufficient lighting to cover your subject and background. Video still has some trouble handling the contrast between well-lit and dark areas - especially following a moving subject. Always ensure that you have enough lights to bring out at least some of the detail in darker areas of your image.

Insider tip #5: Create a recommended clothing list for your models and get in the habit to giving this to your model in advance of the shoot. Things to avoid? White shirts and herringbone patterns – especially for video.

One final point, resist the urge to pan or zoom. If you are a beginner, with starter equipment, you will never be able to pull this off without a slight hesitation at the beginning and a sudden jolt of a stop at the end. I always reject shots like this, the viewer might not be aware of the amateurish movement, but they will think that something is "different" about the shot and it will pull his attention away from the product.

Until you get very good with a video camera, operate it like a still camera with steady, in-focus framing. Let your subject move within your shot, but don't move the camera as you follow them. A slight "pull" of a tripod head will spoil a shot and ruin your chances for a sale. You can also take a close up and a medium shot and edit them together as a "two for one" sale. It's added value to the buyer who can then edit from both shots in whatever manner that they choose. Any time you can add value to a shot, you increase the chances of multiple sales.

6

Make this into your Business

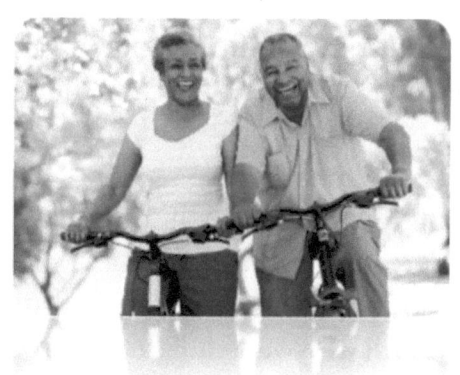

If you want to succeed in microstock, then you need to think about this as a business. Even if you only shoot photographs on one Saturday, every month, set up a schedule. Very simply, you won't be able to measure your success until you get a few dozen photos up on IStock and available to sell. If you're new to photography, your first shoot might only result in two or three photos that you are proud of. Your ability to take more than a handful of quality photos will take some time to develop, so keep at it. You didn't quit after your first day at work so don't quit at this. Make a commitment to place at least 100 photos on IStock. Until you have a sufficient number of photos online, you won't be able to judge your results.

If you've taken my advice, you will have signed up with several microstock agencies at the beginning. As time goes on, you'll find that some agencies do better for you than others. That's why it's important to set up some kind of tracking system from the beginning. An Excel spreadsheet is great, but so is a paperbased system. Keep a month by month record of all your income streams to see where you're making the most money - the results may surprise you.

Many people wonder which microstock agency is the "best". There is no "best". IStockphoto is the biggest, but that doesn't mean that you will make the most money with them. If you read the microstock discussion boards, everyone has a favorite microstock agency (and everyone has complaints about each one), but the best agency for you will be the one which provides you the best income. Remember, you can't judge which microstock company will provide you with the greatest income by their sale price for photos, another company may be able to provide you with more sales which could provide you with better income in the long run.

That leads us to the issue of exclusivtivity. Some of

the stock photo outlets will urge you to become "exclusive" with them and try to sweeten the deal with higher commissions. Your records will allow you to see how your income might be affected if you decided to go exclusive. It's an important decision. All of your photography income will be controlled by one company. In the world of digital sales as a whole, it pays to have many different "streams" come together for your benefit.

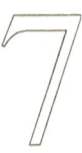

Keep it simple and sell!

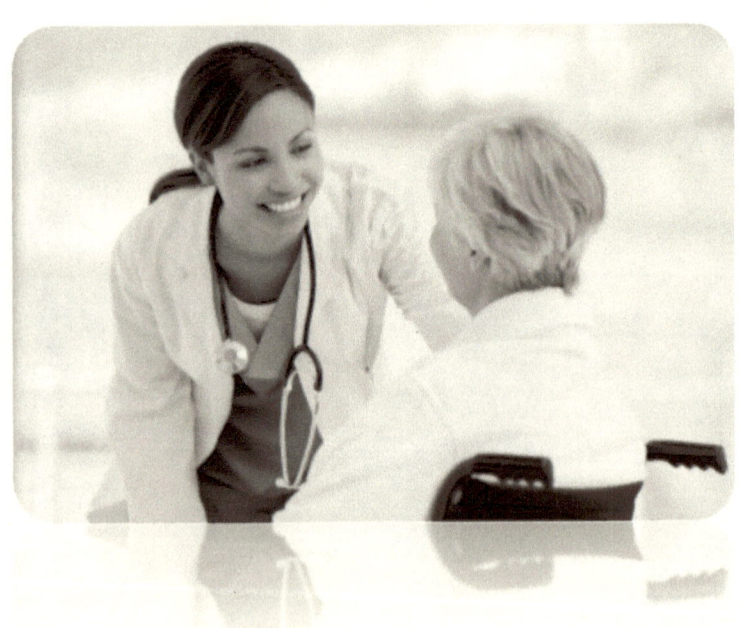

Once you log on to any microstock agency, you'll be able to see photos and videos that cover the wide range of human experience. You might think that anything and everything is fair game - and that's true for submission. For sales, however, it's a whole different matter. The most important thing to remember is that you are here to sell photos. IStock presents it's own warning of things that they have had their fill of - flowers, sunsets, etc.

Most people are putting together brochures for business purposes - so think about what kinds of images appeal to business. Shots of seniors, business transactions, and everyday life always do well. The kinds of things you see all the time. Always ask yourself this question: What could I sell with this photo?

More Tips

If you want to sell photos and videos on IStockphoto, follow these simple rules and you will do fine.

1. **There are certain subjects or areas that you have an advantage in - use that advantage.** If you live in a rural area, you have unique access to farm life shots, harvesting, farm equipment, and pastoral scenes. You already know where the best shots are. Typically, quality shots of American farm life are under-represented. Overall, what niche is available for you. Do you work in a hospital? Are you near a trout stream? Everyone is near something special. If you live 100 miles away from the nearest civilization on a grass prarire, there's a niche you can explore. Decide on what

is special around you. It's a sure bet that you know how to shoot it much better than a visitor would.

2. **Shots that are clearly American.** There are many foreign competitors on IStock and other microstock agencies. They do some wonderful work, but shots taken inside homes or stores look "different". There is a European feel to many of them. It's great work, but it doesn't look like Main Street. Use that as an advantage to create distinctly American shots.

For international photographers, for sure capture images of your own country, but if you are going after the American marketplace, make the photos look distinctly American. Look at the cars parked behind your subject. Look at the construction of nearby buildings.

I see many European shots get it wrong too often, especially when trying to show a business scene. They showcase managers with long hair and European cut suits (which are more form-fitting than American suits). If you are targeting a creative business in America (like ad agencies), those shots might work. But most American managers wear button-down shirts or Polo shirts. In middle-America, the manager's hair is short. That might be a stereotype, but buyers buy stereotypes. They also buy safe. No photo buyer ever got into trouble by buying "safe" images.

3. **Take Shots with faces.** Yes, getting model releases

is a hassle and you may have to do some "convincing" to get friends and family to "pose" for you for free (especially for the second or third time). Most people don't realize how tiring it can become to be a model - especially as a favor. Most photographers try to avoid using people to avoid the hassle of recruitment and model releases. So, to make your photos stand out, include great shots of people. Yes, it's more work, but shots with people will sell more often than similar shots with no people in the frame. People just like to look at people - graphic artists know this and design that way. Use models to stand out from the crowd.

4. Always get a model release. No one is going to buy a shot without a model release. Some Websites allow you to post shots without model releases (IStock is not one of them), but a photo without a release is worthless.

4. **Edit Yourself.** All the microstock agencies are getting overloaded with images. That's because photographers have spent a day out shooting and want to submit everything. The microstock photographer wants to take no chances. Who know what will sell? The trouble is that it's becoming difficult to slog through all the millions of photos on the sites. IStockphoto and other microstock agencies are beginning to remove some photos to better accomodate the buyer. You typically know which will be your best shots and which won't. Do everyone a favor and edit yourself and just submit your best work.

5. **Promote Yourself**

Use a blog or a Website to promote your work. Write
about the kind of images that you sepecialize in. Link
to your work on IStockphoto. Learn to use keywords to
help searchers find your photo. Just because it's easy to
upload images doesn't mean you can stop thinking
about the business side of photography. Also, use the
forums and social networking tools on IStockphoto to
get traffic to your work. The more people who see your
images the greater chance that you have to make a sale.

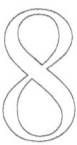

David Lewis

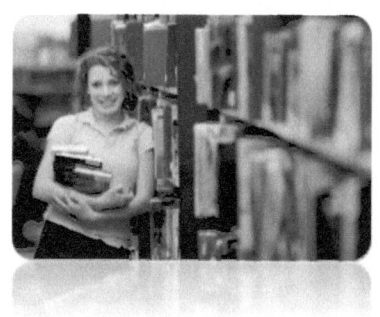

At the beginning of this tutorial, I mentioned my friend David Lewis - one of IStockphoto's most successful photographers. He has a variety of interests, and photography is only one of them. He started on IStock has an outlet for his hobby and he was stunned by his results. Here is an except from an interview I conducted with David almost two years ago. He discusses two of the more successful photographs that he had in his portfolio at that time. Please note how simple these top earning photos are. A photo of the American flag and a shot of his daughter at the library. Some of the stats that Davis lists are old. He how has over 2,600 images on IStockphoto and the shot of his daughter has sold over 1,000 times!

So, let David speak for himself!

"The first one (above) is my most frequent seller of all of the 980 images in my portfolio. It went up Feb. 25 and has sold 131 times, or an average of 95 sales a month. My 15-year-old daughter needed to do some research at the downtown library one Sunday afternoon, so I told her I'd take her if she'd work with me on a few photos there. Got several keepers out of it, and she found the books she needed. Win win!"

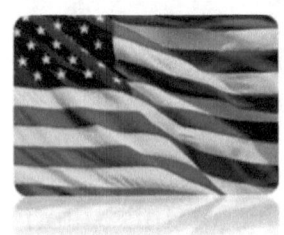

"The second one, the American flag, has been up since October 2006. I was actually doing a shoot for a client -- something I do very little of since I have a full-time day job -- that day at some apartments in Benton, Arkansas, and they had this gorgeous, enormous American flag on display. It was a beautiful sunny day with lots of wind, so I shot maybe 30 frames of this flag looking for one like this. This one has sold 299 times,

times, averaging 45 sales a month."

As a reminder, these are old figures for David's sales reports. You can see more of David's work – and current sales – on IStockphoto.David has put of plenty more photos since then, but these photos continue to be top sellers for him. That's the great thing about IStock, you can continue to sell the same photos year after year.To see more of David's work, log on to IStockphoto. He is "dlewis33".

Microstock Diaries

Of course, David Lewis is an exception. If you want to read the microstock blog of another person who uploads to microstock, check out Microstock Diaries on the Web. Lee Torrens describes himself as a hobbyist photographer who has been uploading images for several years now. He reports on his total earnings each month from the various microstock sites that he uses. In August of 2009, he reported monthly earnings of over $700 each month. Torrens takes the time to consider the "sell through" rates of each of his photos and average income per photo. You can't help but read this blog and become very knowledgeable about the business of microstock.

Photos That Work
I'm not a photographer, but I'm a photo buyer. I've bought hundreds of photos for hundreds of publications. It may surprise photographers, to know that I'm not looking for the most beautiful shot, but more for the

shot that's clearly about an idea and helps me explain a product or service. For example:

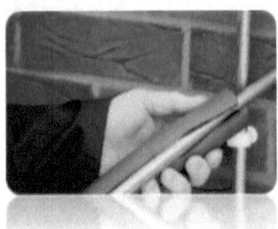

There's nothing pretty about the shot above. But, if your trying to create a brochure about home insulation (especially pipe insulation), then this is a shot that is right on target. Now, with a lot of government stimulus money available, there will be more and more demand for these types of photos. It always pays to be part of something that has a lot of money behind it and this photo can ride that wave. Critics might prefer that it be shot against a white background so that the image will "POP". However, on the day I was searching for images, this was the only one available, so I bought it. By now, there might be a hundred more photos about energy efficience (including pipe insulation) on IStock. Successful photographers are always searching the marketplace trying to discover the next big thing. Being first in the marketplace can pay big dividends, so always try to arrive to the part early!

Ride the Wave

We've seen this couple before…

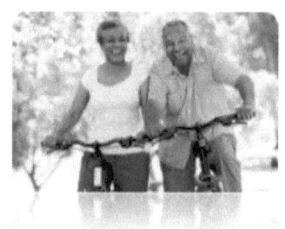

They are part of the big wave of baby boomers facing retirement over the next decade. Billions of dollars will be targeted to this affluent, important market. I used this image for a brochure that I was working on, went to lunch and spotted it, cropped, on a bus stop. It will probably be used a hundred or more times over the next decade and this smiling couple will be paying the photographer for his trouble many times over.

What makes this image remarkable? It can used for health related topics (another issue with money behind it) and for successful aging, and retirement planning. All of those subjects will require a great deal of promotion for many more years.

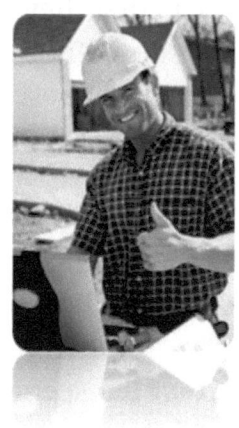

Could this be an easier shot or more basic? But look at home many ways that it could be used. It has a market for new home construction, heating and cooling, home improvements, employement, good health, the economy, and many other products. More important, millions of dollars are spent each year promoting those products. These are the kind of phtos that you want to submit to IStockphoto.

Remember in all of this, think about the photo shoot (your potential competitor) that you want to replace. What does your future customer want to sell? Can you shoot the kind of images that will help him or her reach that goal? You will become successful on IStockphoto in porportion to your ability to help others reach their goals. Don't just glance at top-selling photos - study them. Why are they so successful?What kind of images will your prospects need that will help them sell their products? Most frequently, the reason that people don't succeed in microstock is that they put up hundreds of random images on the site without a clear idea of what kinds of products or services these images will support. Don't let that be you.

I tried to select average photos for this book. Shots that anyone could take and sell for stock photography. These are shots that you can take as well. You don't need to be a great photographer, just help people sell products and ideas – that the secret of stock photography.

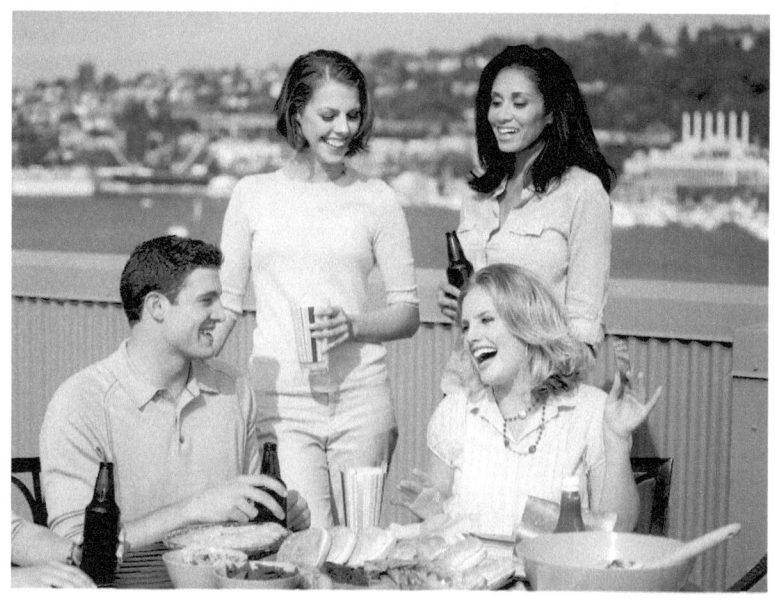

See the above photo? Anyone could take it, nice location, but nothing extraordinary. These are the kind of shots that people are turning into a great source of secondary income. As you turn all the online photo sites, you'll see great photos that are breathtaking in scope and artistry. However, the overwhelming number of photos you'll see are like the images in this book – workmanlike. Don't be intimidated by the top photographers, keep your eye on your goal – a great source of income that will pay you year after year.

9

Don't Wait

Don't wait to get started, start right now. I don't mean for you to grab a camera and head out the door – although don't let me stop you. I like ambition and confidence. Now is the time to begin thinking about your first shoot. Log on to all the microstock sites and begin reading the forums. Ask questions. The photographers on these forums are especially helpful to "newbies". I will list some sites for you to check out in the final pages of this book.

Also, do some Web searches with the keyword phrase "microstock blog". Many photographers are openly blogging about their success in microstock and posting their monthly sales results. You'll probably notice that the most successful photographers have hundreds on images online. Find a photographer that shoots the kind of subjects that you are interested in and post questions to his or her blog. Photographers will always be your best resource as you build your on-line portfolio.

I hope this book has been of help to you in getting started. I've approached it from a "get started now" and "don't waste money" until you know it works stand-point. It's important to me to save money until you know this is right for you. A photographer would prob-ably give you advice on cameras and lens and lights. You'll get a lot of advice as you begin in microstock, you'll have to filter all of it through your own expe-rience and values. I do know, however, that with persistence, anyone can add excellent income to their household budget through microstock. It's a great fi-nancial resource for cash-strapped families. I'm looking forward to seeing you on IStockphoto!

Other Sites for Photos and Video

IStockphoto
Shutterstock
Always HD
Pond 5
Revostock
ClipDealer
Fotolia
Getty Images
Bigstockphoto
Stockxpert
Microstock blogs

Microstock Diaries
Microstock Blog
Microstockphoto
Arcurs

www.ingramcontent.com/pod-product-compliance
Lightning Source LLC
Chambersburg PA
CBHW021043180526
45163CB00005B/2260